Happy 30th Birthday!
Celebrate You!
Adult Coloring Book

By Peaceful Mind Adult Coloring Books

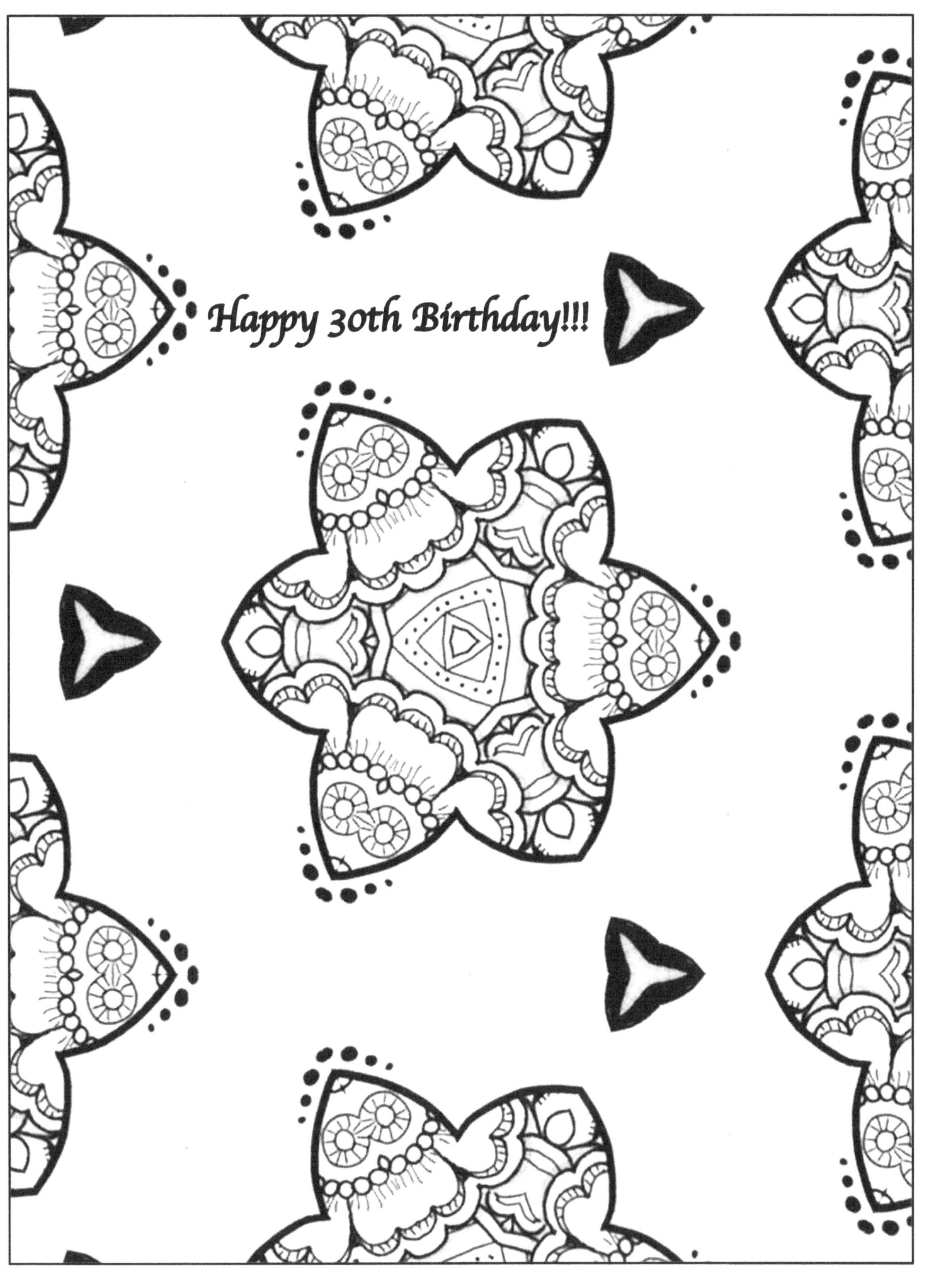

Happy 30th Birthday!!!

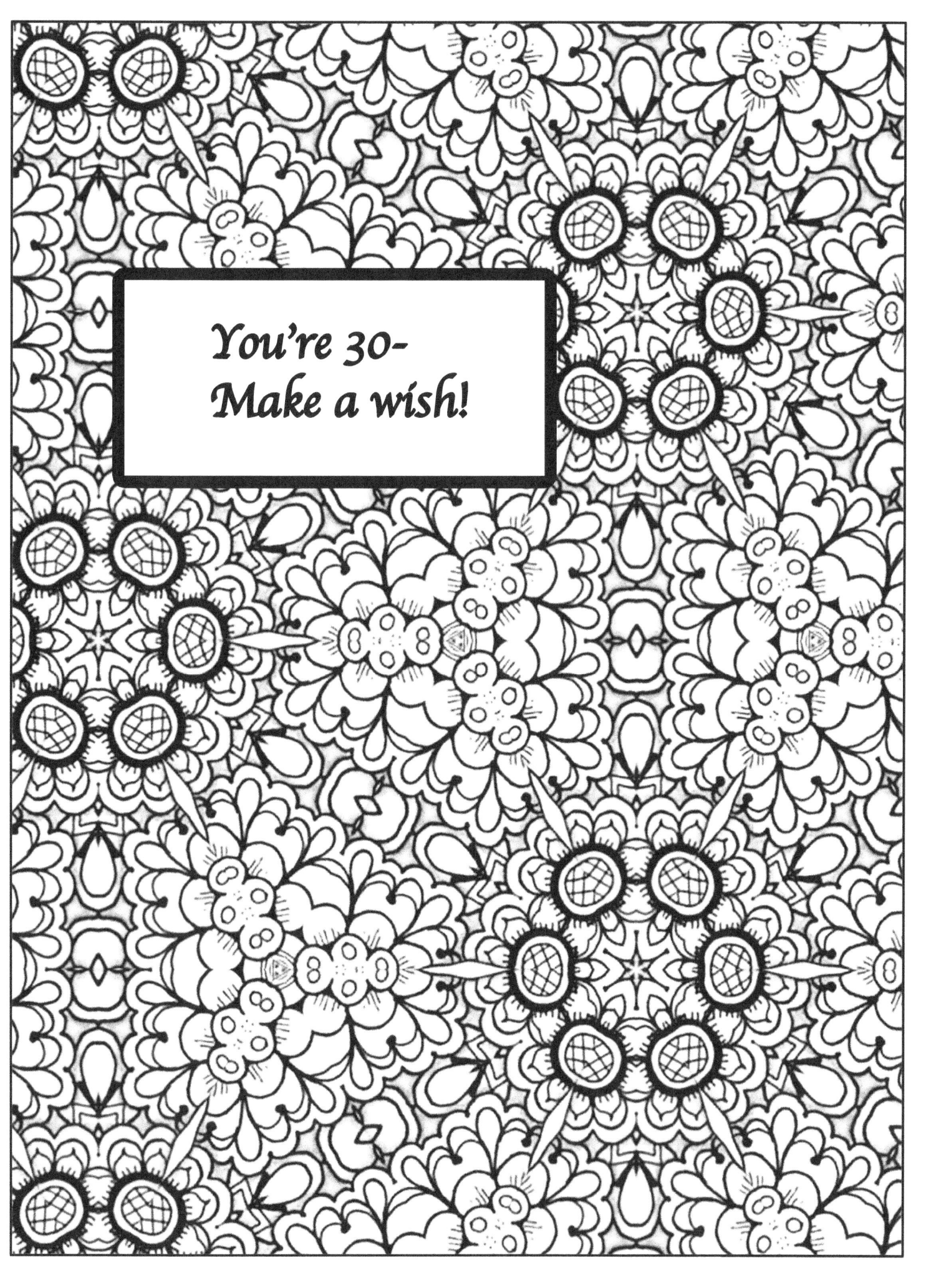

You're 30-
Make a wish!

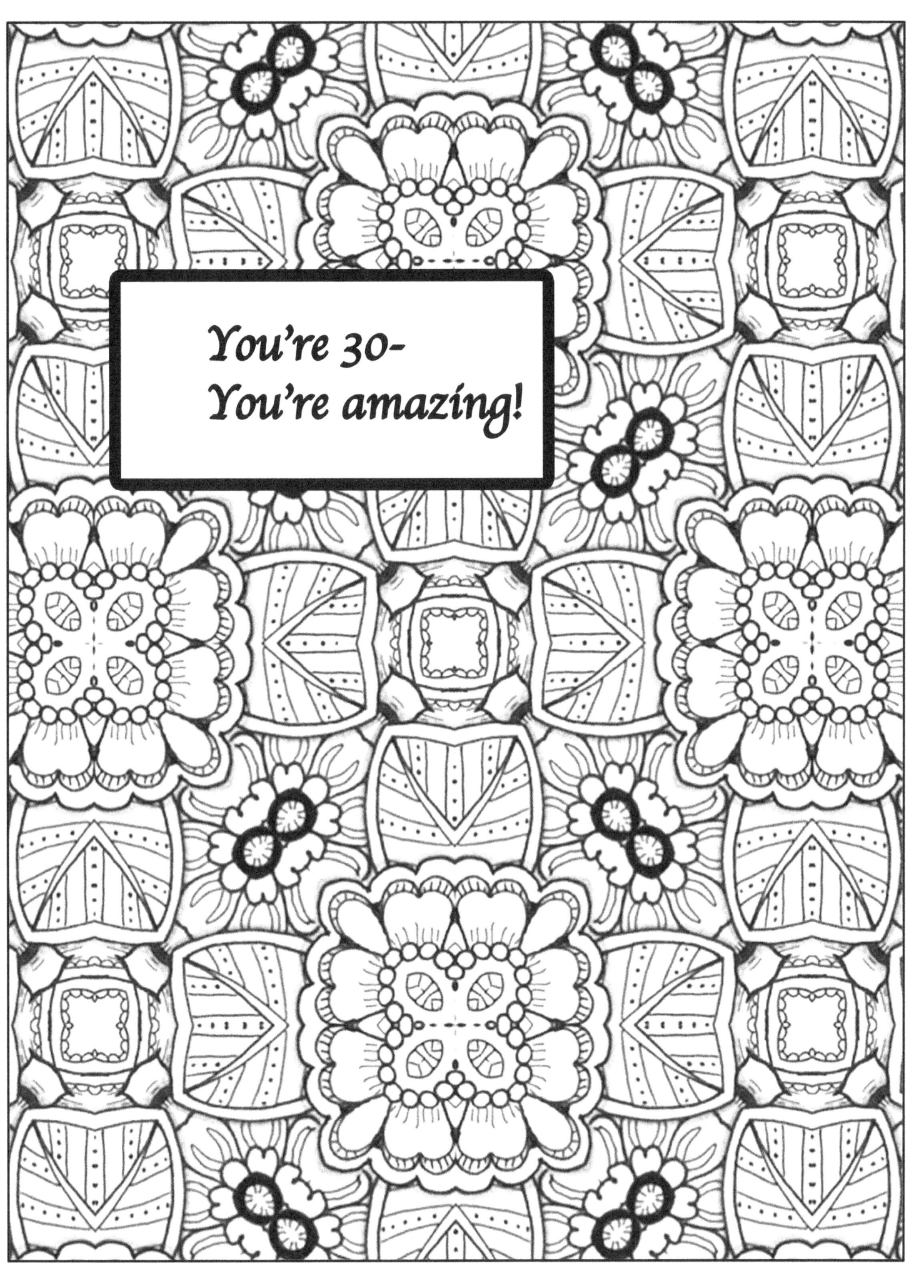

You're 30-
You're amazing!

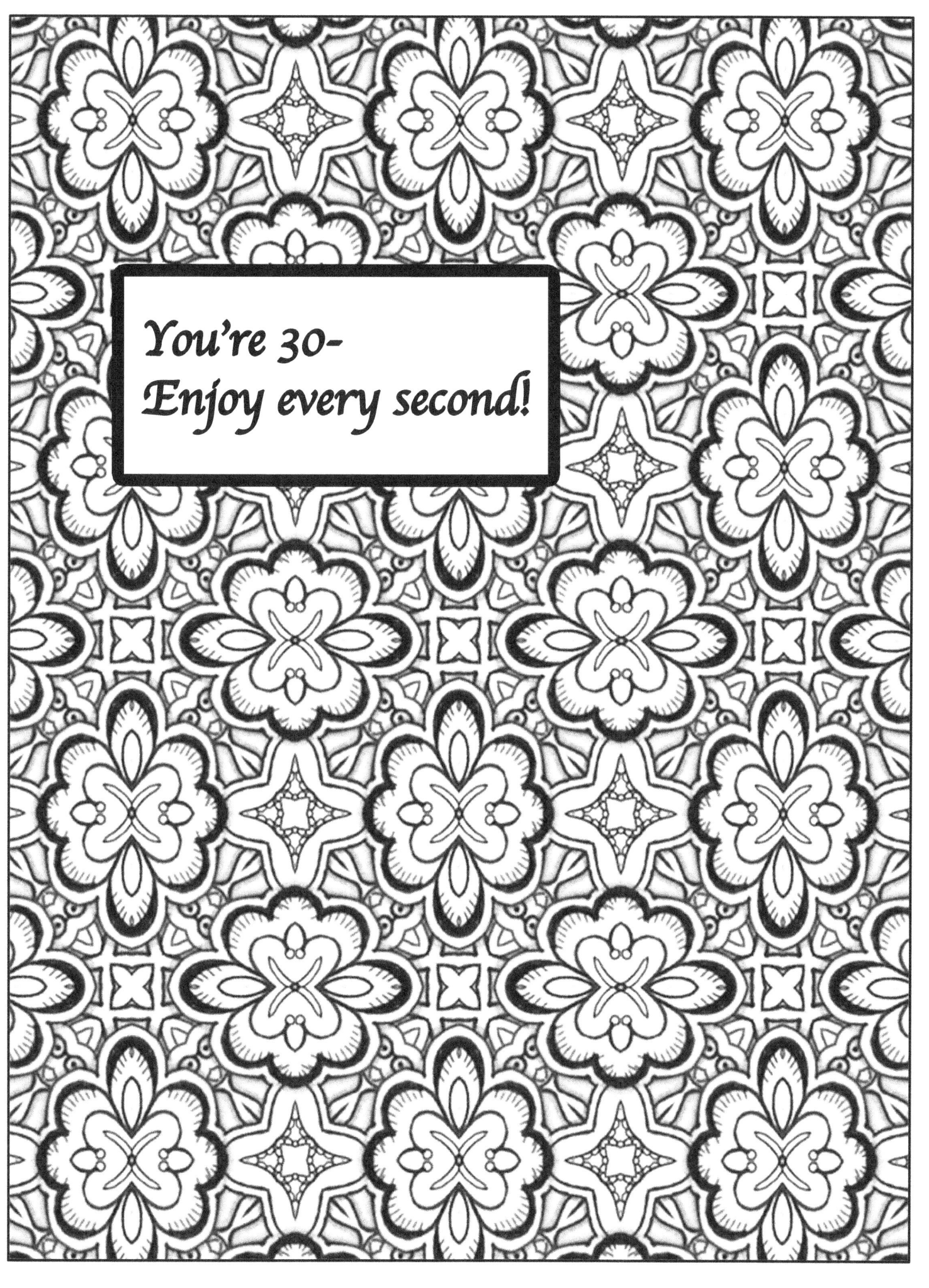

You're 30-
Enjoy every second!

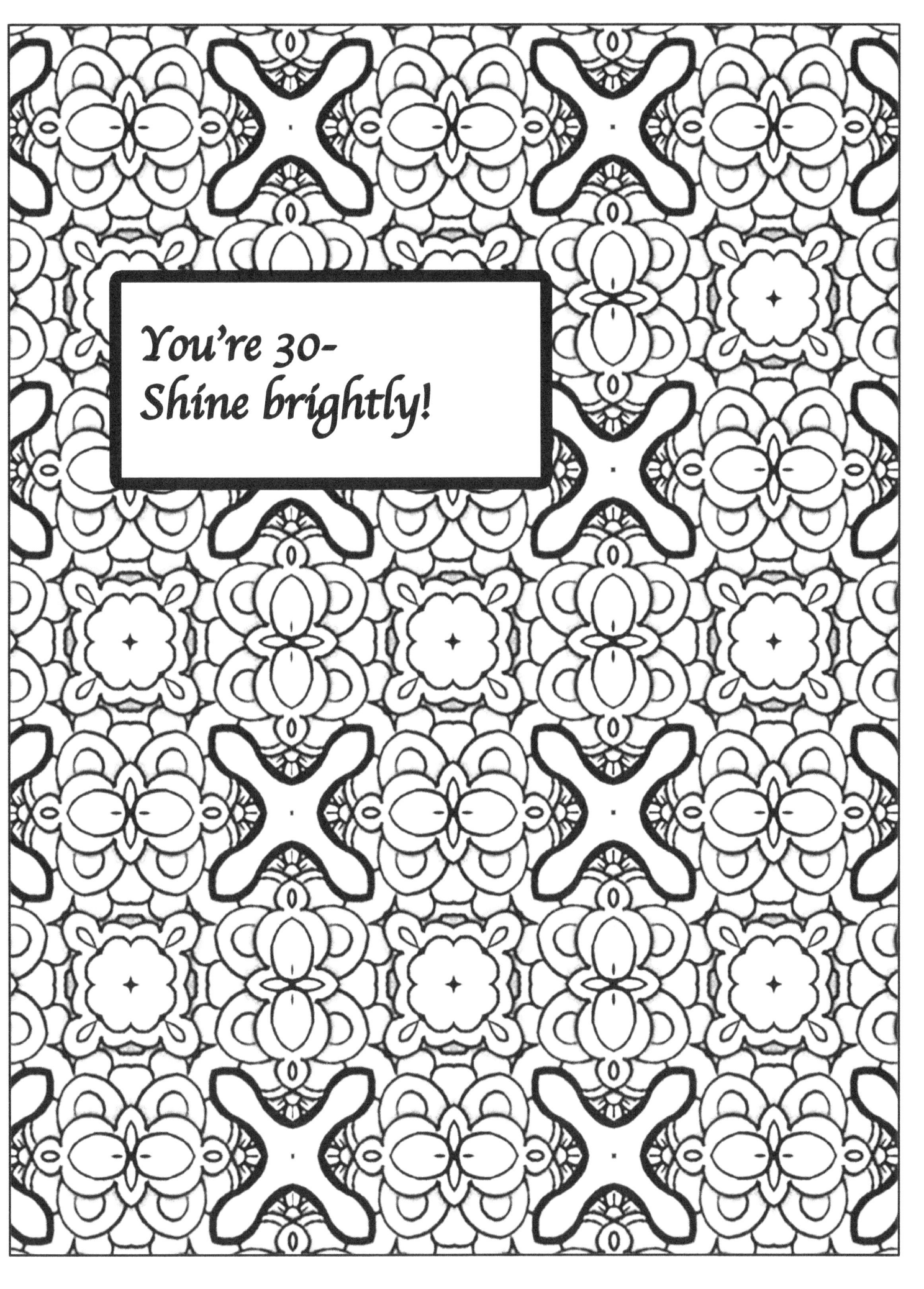

You're 30-
Shine brightly!

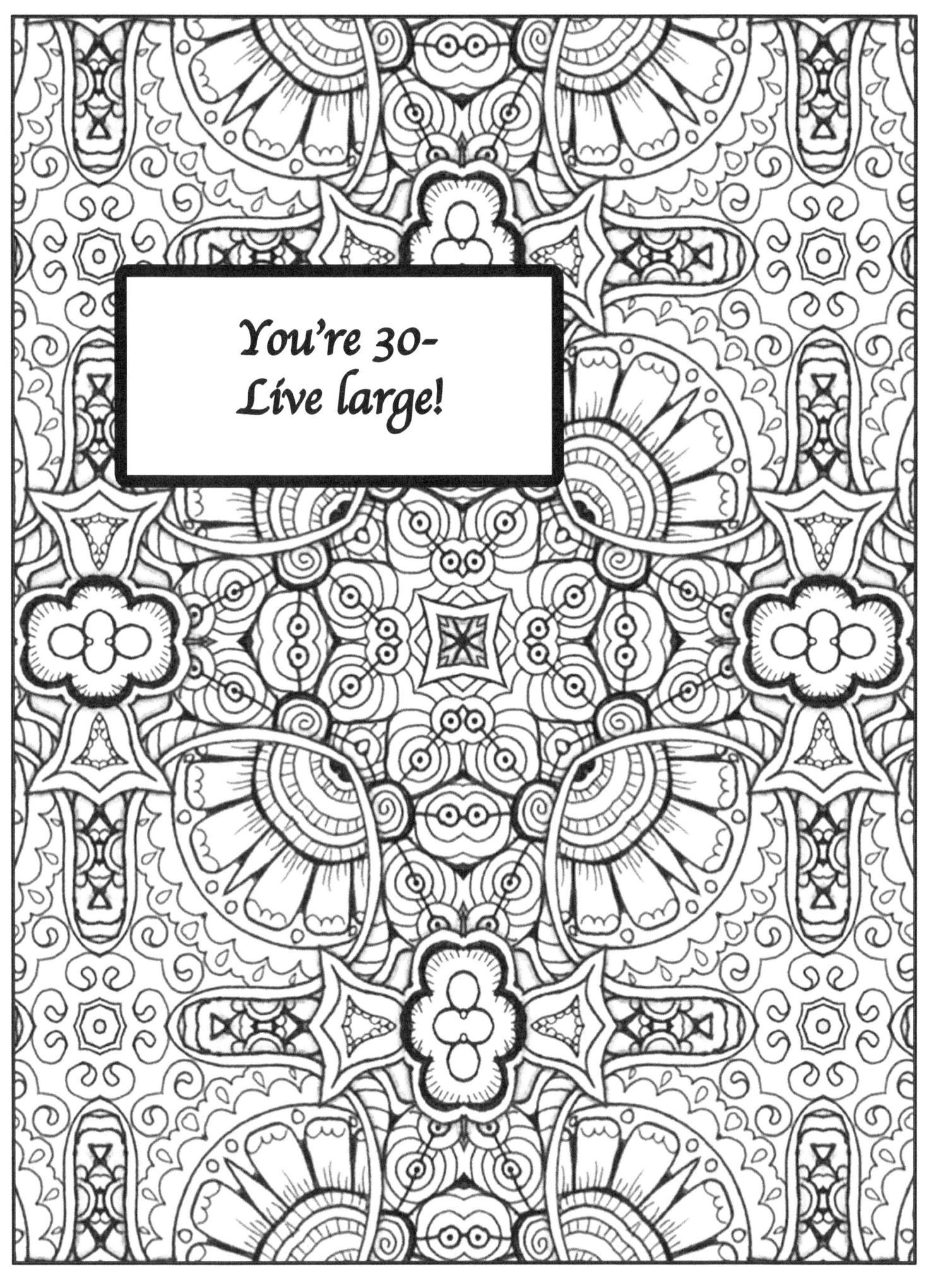

You're 30-
Live large!

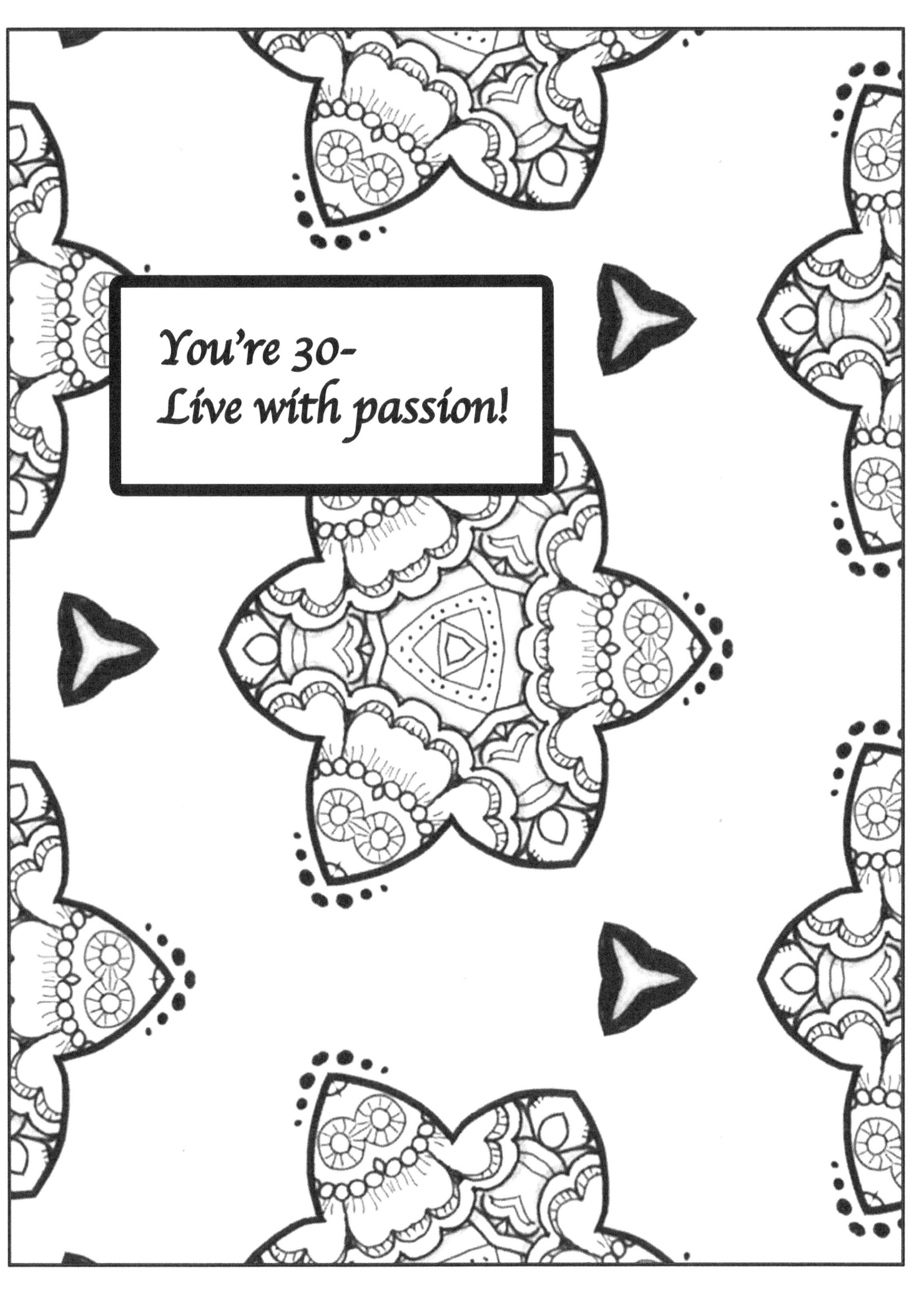

You're 30-
Live with passion!

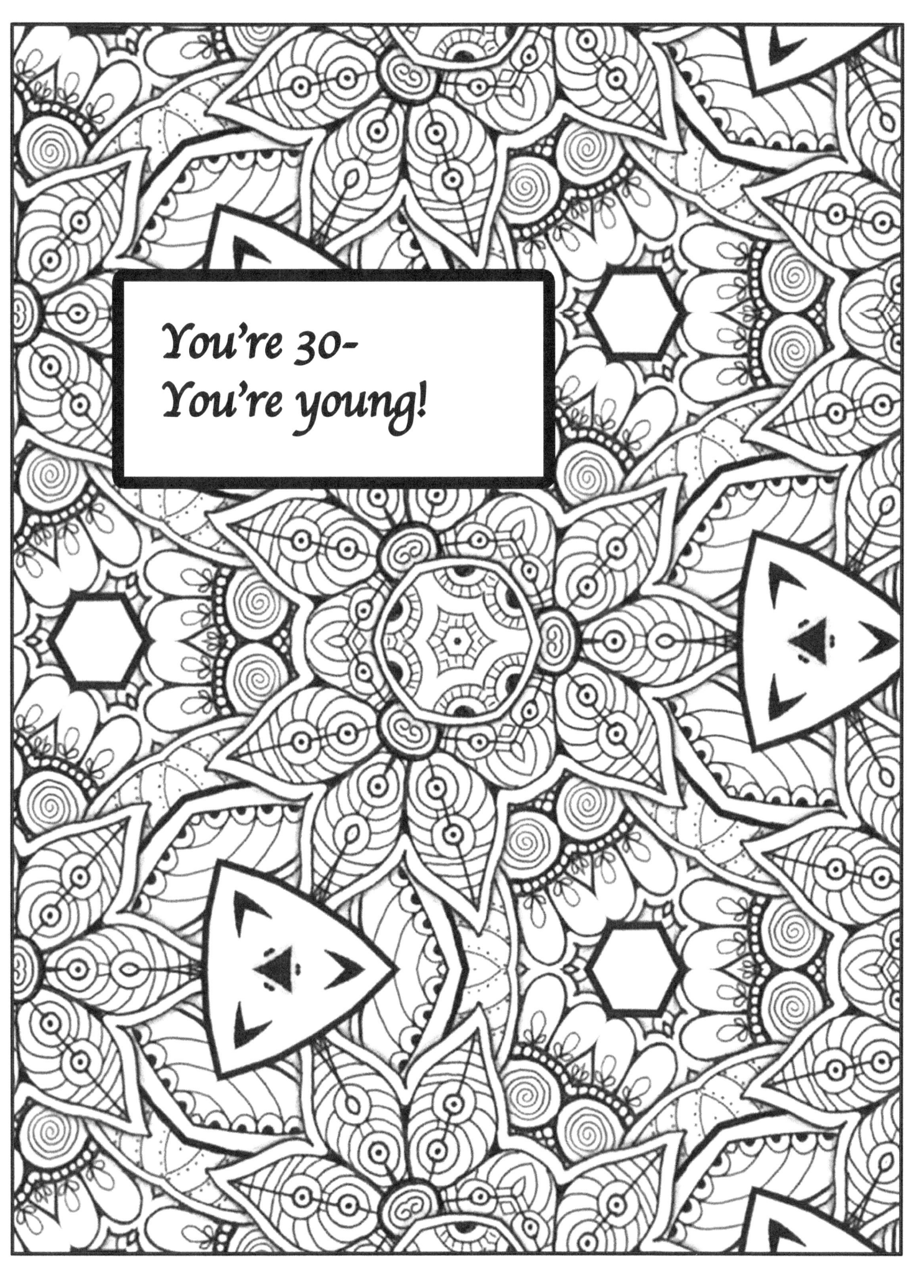

You're 30-
You're young!

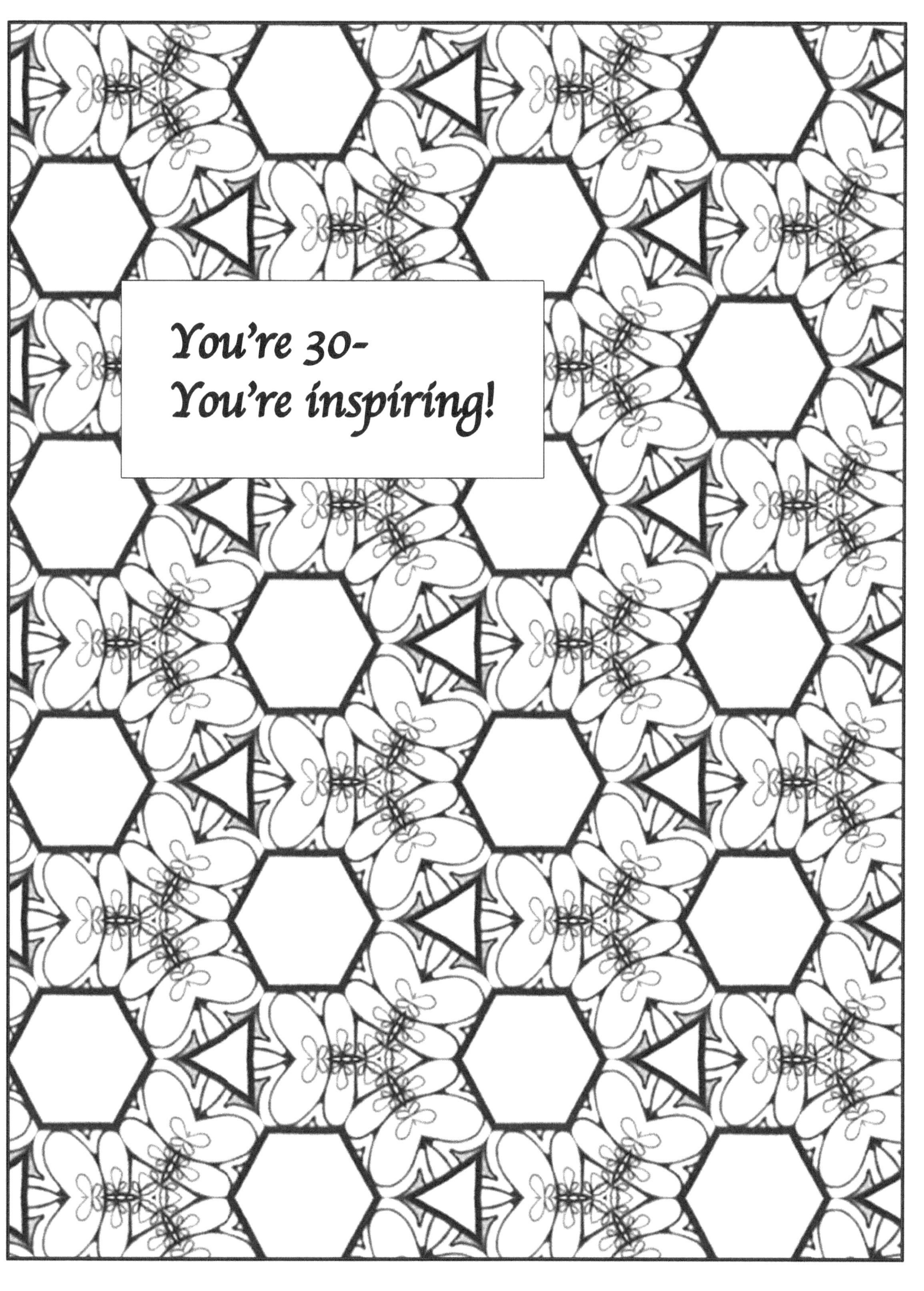

You're 30-
You're inspiring!

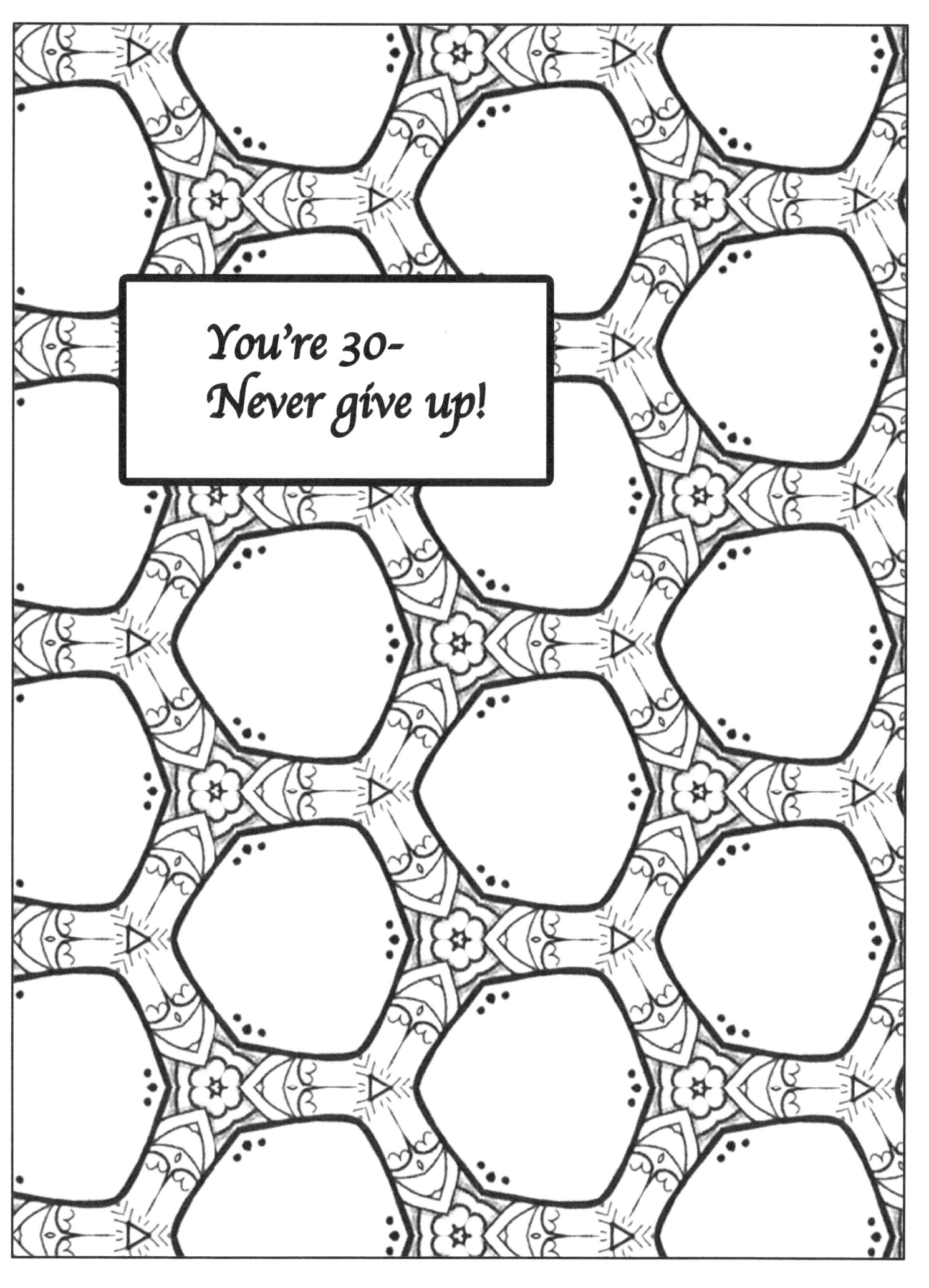

You're 30-
Never give up!

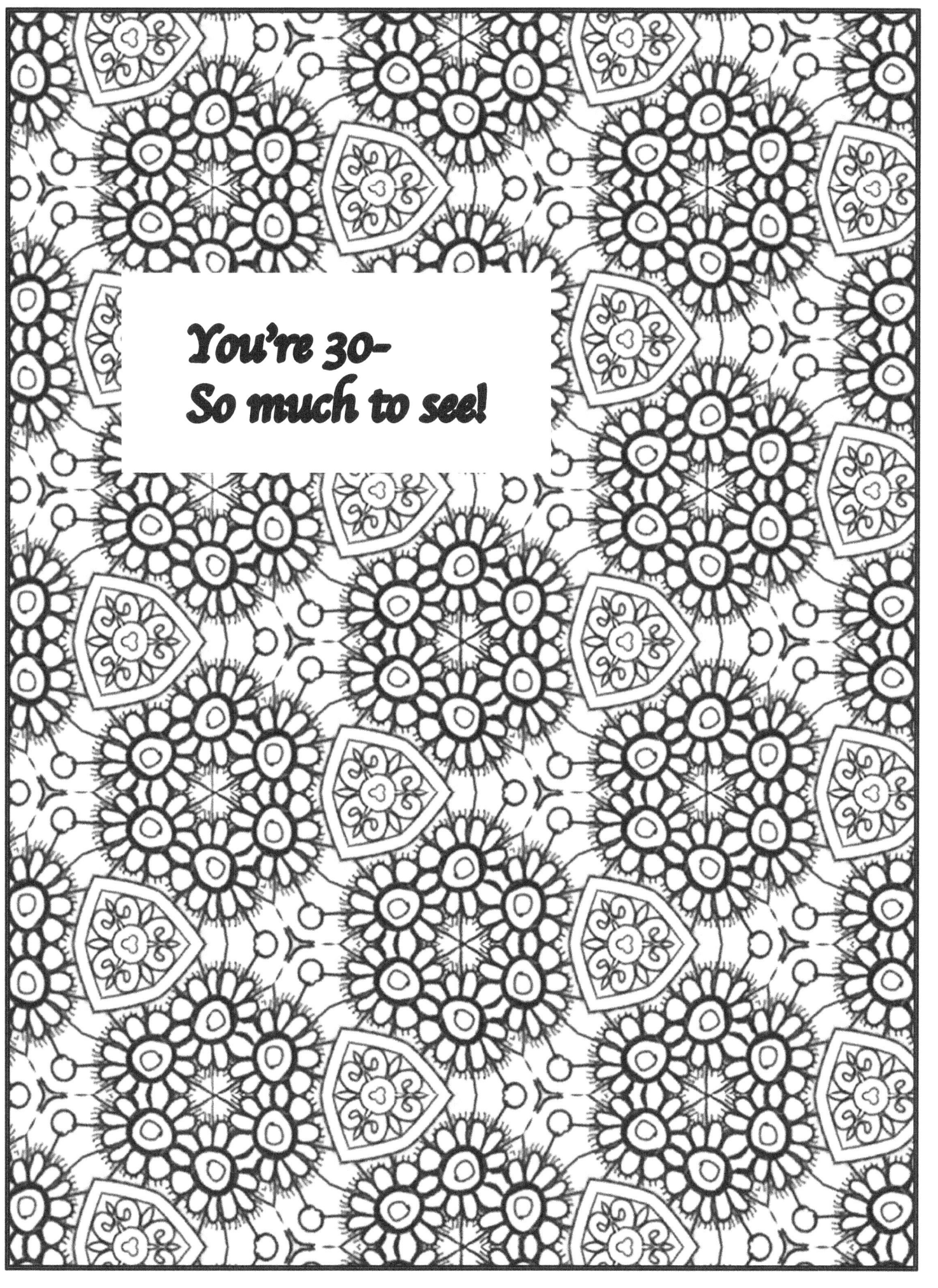

You're 30–
So much to see!

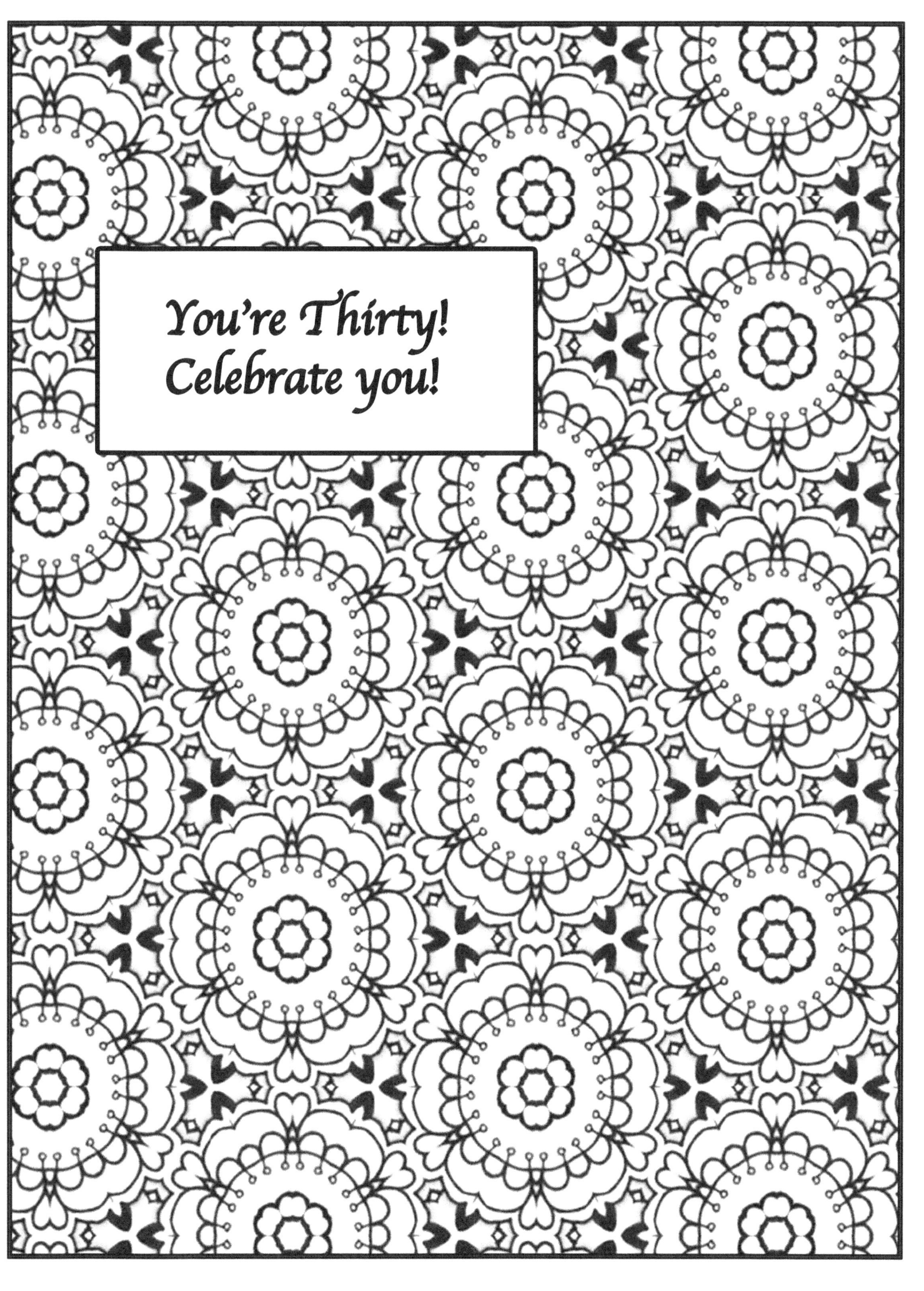

You're Thirty!
Celebrate you!

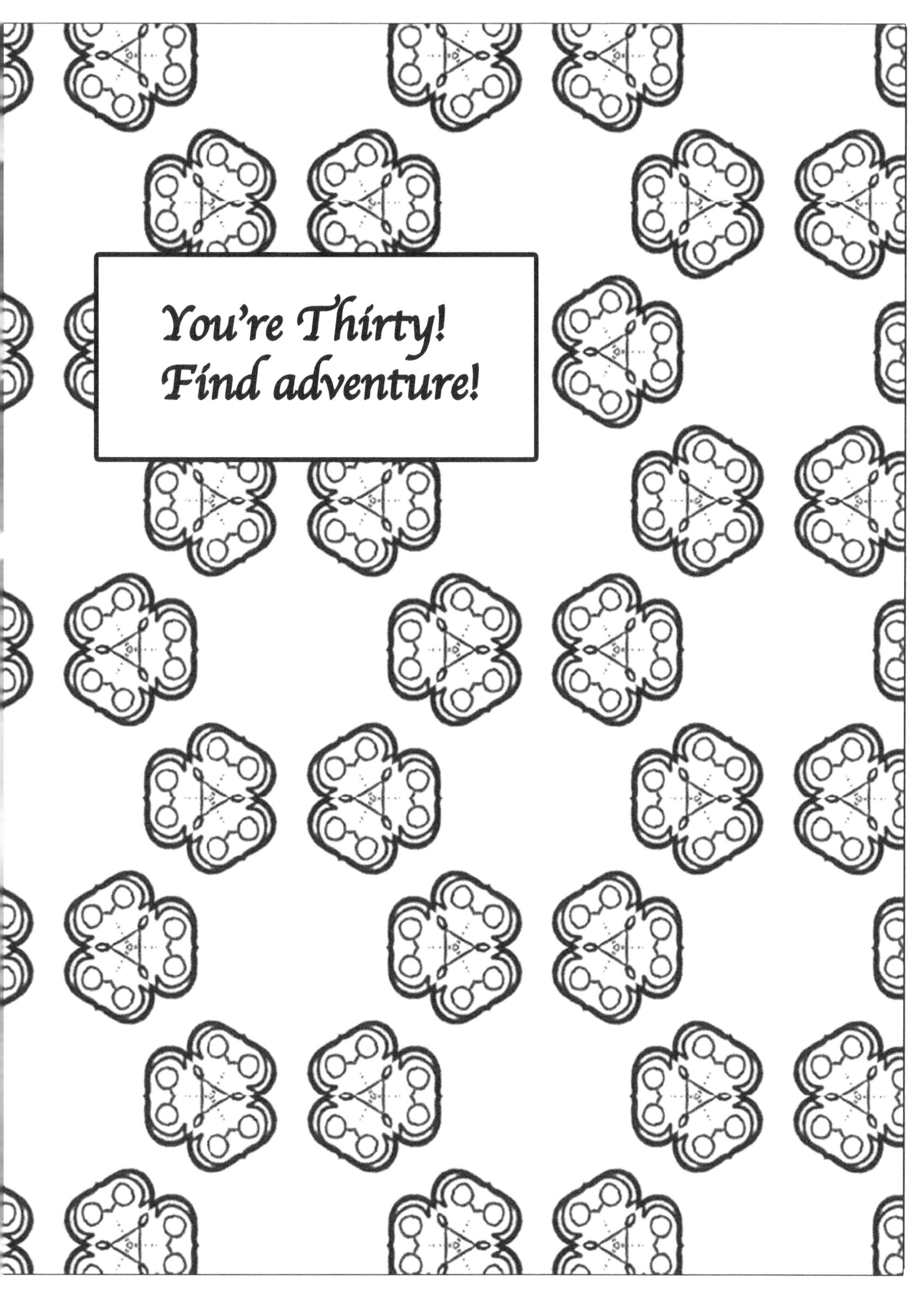

You're Thirty!
Find adventure!

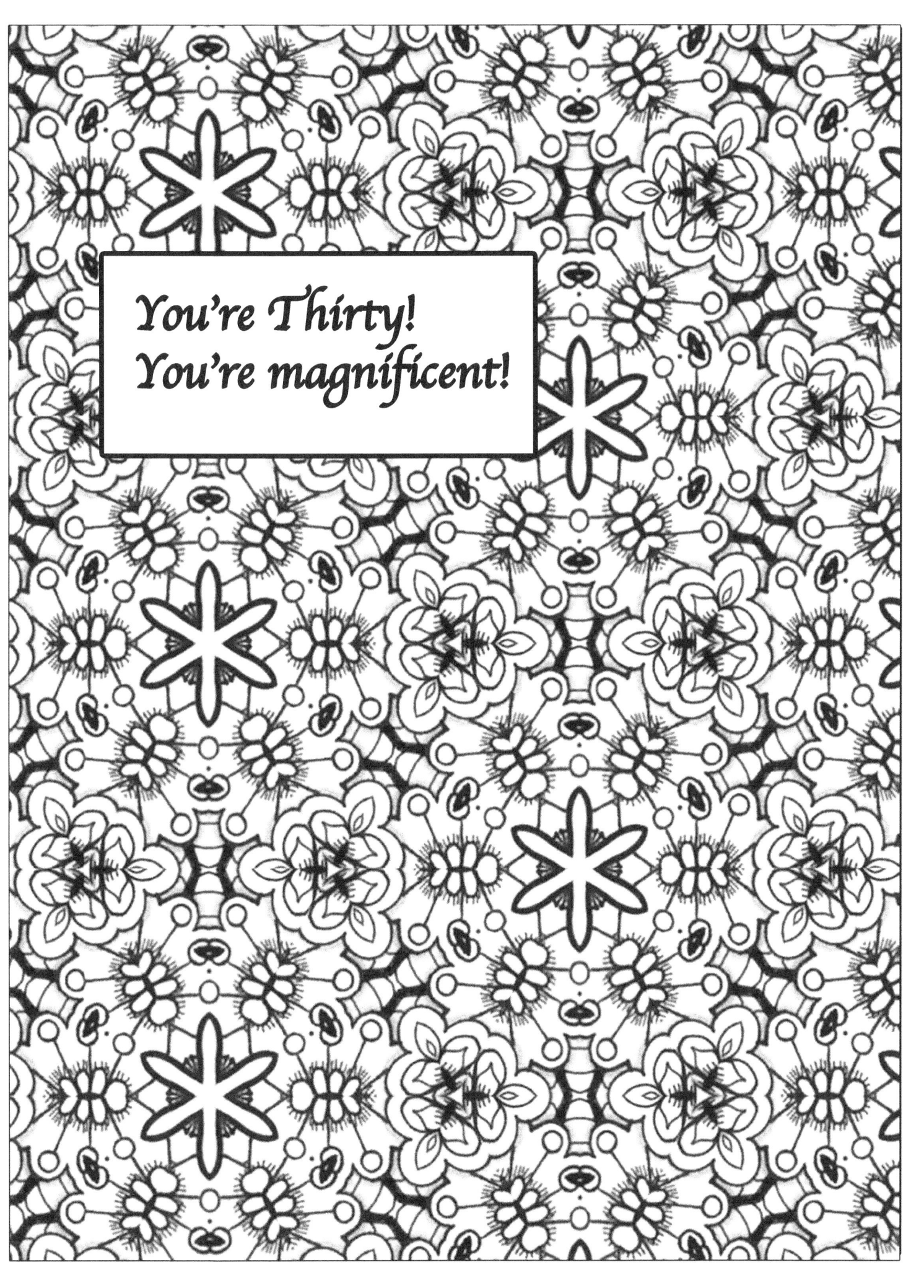

You're Thirty!
You're magnificent!

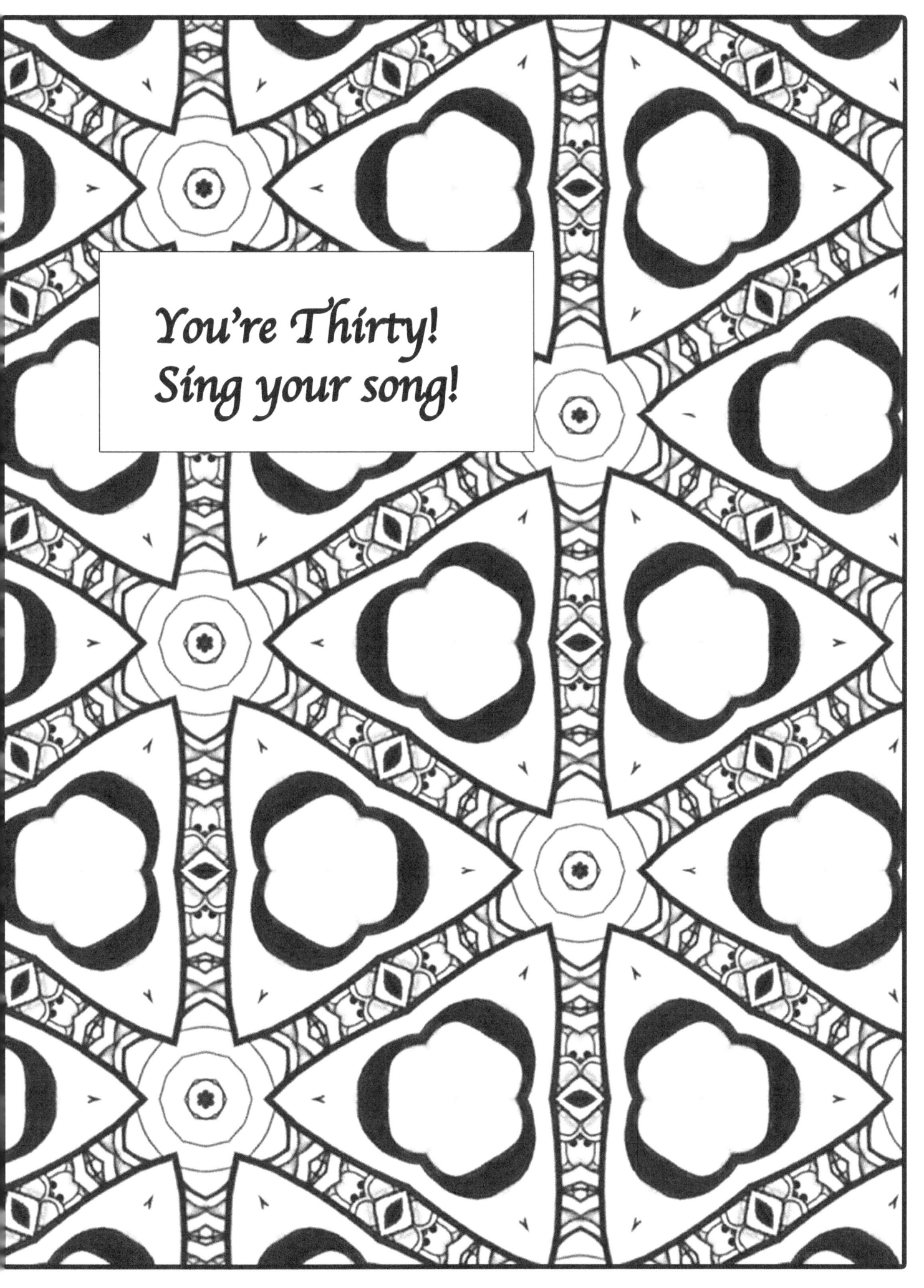

You're Thirty!
Sing your song!

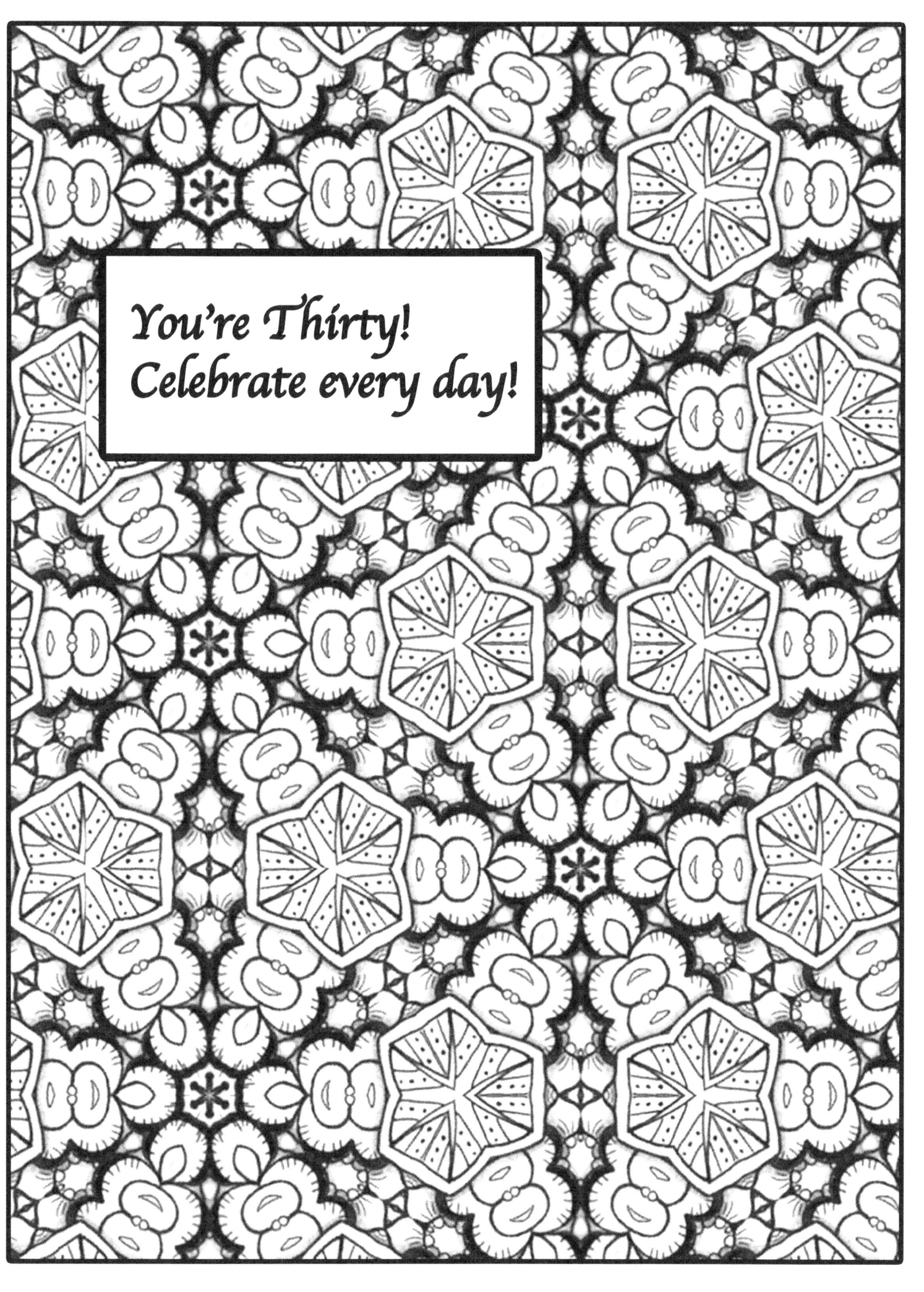

You're Thirty!
Celebrate every day!

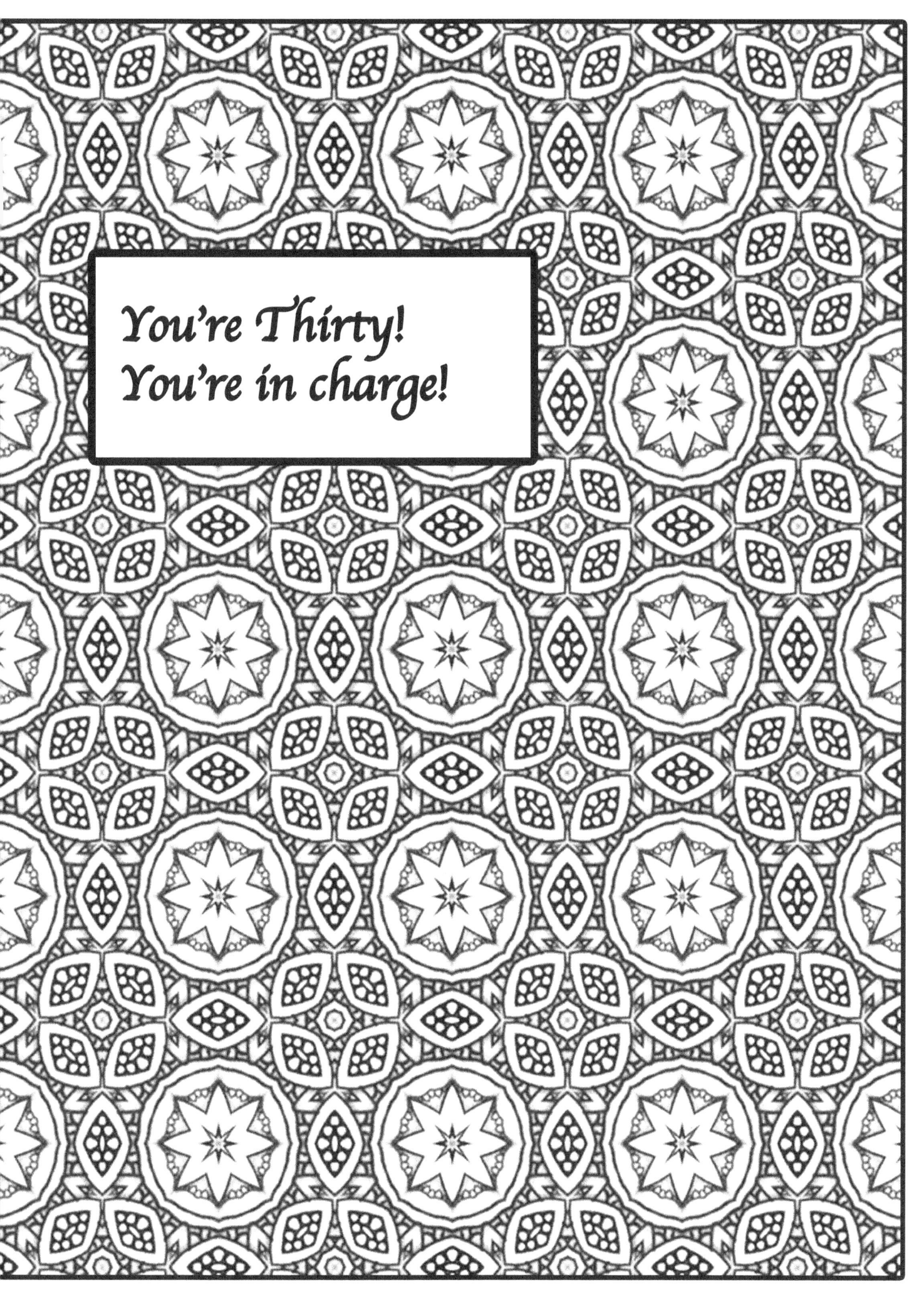

You're Thirty!
You're in charge!

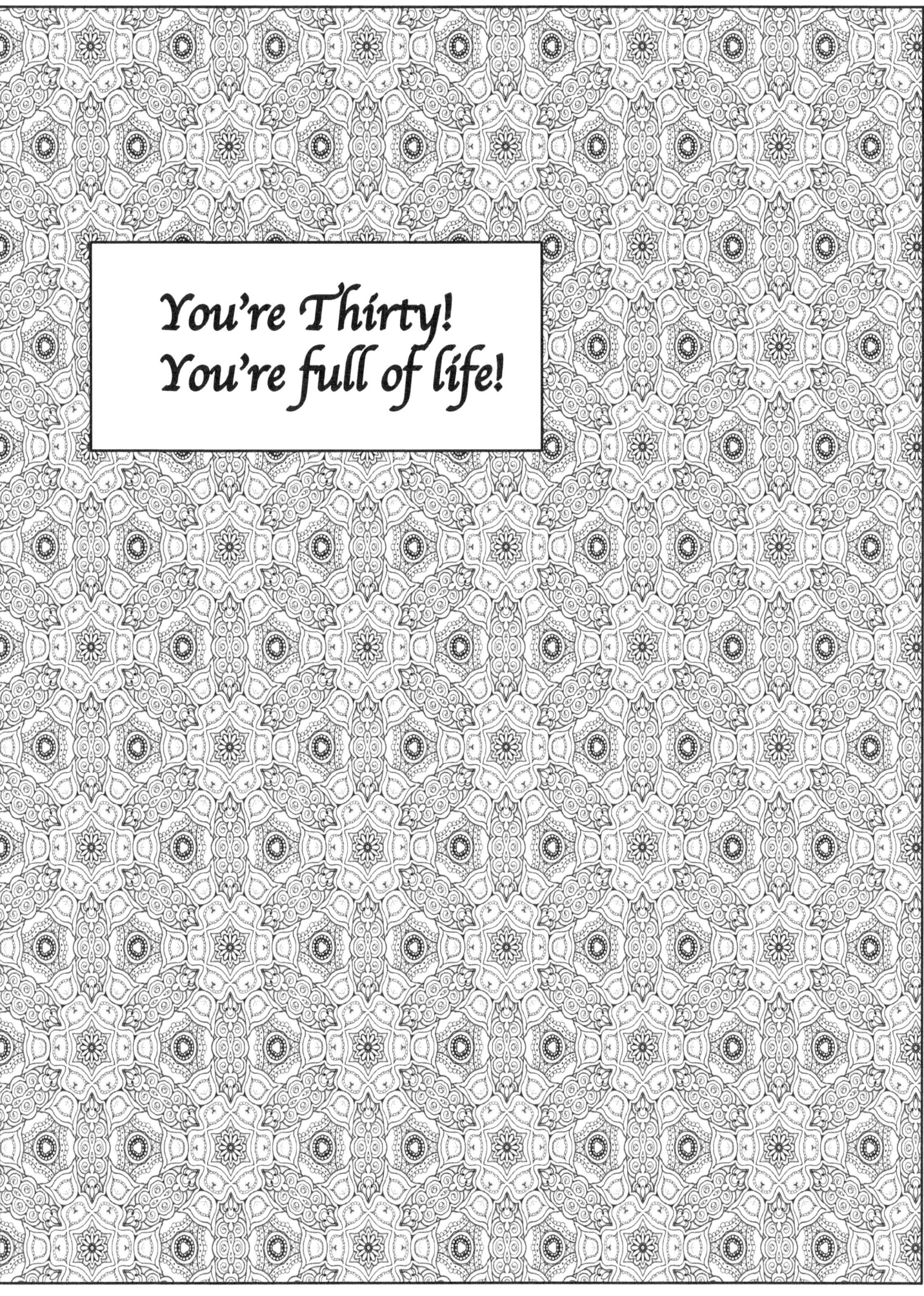

You're Thirty!
You're full of life!